INTERNATIONAL BEST SELLING AUTHOR

GET INSPIRED

GET INSPIRED, GET LIFE

HELEN N. YOGO

GET INSPIRED

A Publication of
PRECIOUS BELOVED EVANGELICAL
MISSION WORLDWIDE

helenpangout@gmail.com
ladyyogo@yahoo.com
Skype: yogolistic
Facebook: Precious Beloved Emw
Instagram: hellymissy

ISBN: 978-978-60675-0-6

Printed by
Colour Tech Prints
16, Thomas Salako Street, Ogba, Lagos
Tel: 08023544938, 08169052667

DEDICATION

This book is dedicated to all who have stayed long enough in the wilderness of pain, torment, suffering, neglect, and want and are looking for answers, I say, don't give up; your case is unique and special. God will lead you there if you look up to Him, hold on, and do not rely on your own understanding.

PREFACE

Thousands of talents, potentials, initiatives, strategies, dreams, and goals that were never realized, accomplished, shared, enacted, and achieved have been recorded in graveyards. Because of fear of the unknown, criticism, and a lack of self-confidence, some people die without expressing their God-given talents and abilities.

Get Inspired is a tool for everyone. It is a book of encouragement that can be carried with you. It teaches that as long as one has life, not all hope is lost. It goes a long way toward inspiring its readers to be inspired to be creative, take initiative, and make the most of their lives.

We all need help, as stated in this book, but the specific help you require is within you. No one will ever be able to assist you sufficiently, and above all, God is the only Faithful Helper at all times, imploring us to work, watch, and pray.

This small book appears to be a blessing to every reader, and it will rouse those who have been sleeping and waiting to awaken.

Enjoy this work and consider what you can do to help others appreciate and remember that they were once you.

Do not die unknown, do not pass through this life as a no body, and do not consider your background or environment because it has no bearing on the success that God has planned for you. **NO MORE SLEEPING, GET INSPIRED, AND INSPIRE YOUR LIFE.**

ACKNOWLEDGMENT

I want to thank God Almighty (who I refer to as My God of Surprises) for investing so much in me in order to announce me. Merci Seigneur!

I am grateful to my family for putting up with me, encouraging me not abandoning me during my seasons of personal struggles.

Though I conceived and wrote this book in 2010 during my postgraduate studies at Ahmadu Bello University in Zaria, Kaduna State, Nigeria, it was published in 2024. My heartfelt gratitude goes to my glorious husband, Prince A.G.Bertrand Ndjonte Pangout, and our blessed children, Princesses Happiness Domkam, Holiness Mbohngho, Heavenly Njimfock, and Haniella Nguemdjo for their unending love.

I am grateful to my mentor, Mr Paul Agbih of Germany, Late Professor Anomah Ngu of Cameroon, and General Abayomi Zamba (who unfortunately died on the 25/12/2023) of Nigeria for their positive influences.

I acknowledge Mr. Adetunji Adebowale.A. Moses, for encouraging me to belief in myself. And for Mr. Suresh Khatri of India for first reading through my work in 2013.

My gratitude goes to everyone in Nigeria, India, and Cameroon who supported the success of this long awaited book. My apologies for not mentioning all names.

I also acknowledge those who, knowingly or unknowingly, contributed to my pains and sufferings, because it was during those times of wants, desperation, neglect, lack, frustration in tears, day and night, that God showed me what I had in me and how I could better use my time rather than lamenting on what will not increase me but will cause me more pain. It is sometimes beneficial to go through situations because they serve as a propelling force to your promised land.

GRATITUDE

I remain grateful to Mommy Apostle Akin-Salami Ope And Daddy Pastor Salami Ibidapo Akinjide for their tiredness support and prayers in cementing the success publication of this book.

Our heartfelt gratitude to Mr Abiodun Sobola and Brother Michael Kehinde for the technicalities of this work. May the Lord mightily bless the works of their hands.

INTRODUCTION

Oh, how wonderful are His Handiwork! What a rewarding experience it is to discover your talent or gift. After going through a lot of painful experiences in this life and having no one to lend a helping hand when I needed it the most, I understand what others are going through in life, so I decided to use God's vision to inspire and brighten people's days, faces and encourage them to persevere until God says He is tired of their cases, which will never happen because God is never tired of blessing His children. Because God did not allow me to fail, no one who reads and ponders the inspirational words in this book will either.

This book is also a meditation and reflection guide, as well as a discernment and critical self-check for all people in the world. As you read Get Inspired, may you be blessed.

Above all, my main vision for writing this book, which was guided by God through the Holy Spirit of God who gives wisdom, is to raise others and tell them that they are very important and are a fundamental part of this world. This book can also be given as a gift to someone when the giver is at a loss for what to give on a special occasion. It will put a smile on a tired face and be a good companion when traveling so that you are not bored.

GET INSPIRED

I'd appreciate it if you could respond with any observations, critiques, or recommendations about this book or any other of mine you've read.

That is perfectly acceptable.

Author

Muertoh(Princess) Nohgwe H. Y.

helenpangout@gmail.com

ladyyogo@yahoo.com

Skype: yogolistic

Facebook: Precious Beloved Emw

Instagram: hellymissy

CONTENT

GET INSPIRED

GET INSPIRED

MORNING

A morning is a symbol of a new day on Earth.

It indicates that God has given you another day to make amends for your mistakes in the past.

The sun shines brighter in the morning.

That is how your life should be.

Living is a gain.

However, to die is to lose.

It is wonderful to be alive.

Every morning, begin with your Source and Creator.

And become a Champion

DAYS

Every day is unique.

Monday is not a Tuesday or a Wednesday,

And it will never be a Thursday or a Friday.

As a result, if this Tuesday isn't going well,

Remember that there will be another Saturday and Sunday.

Never give up hope,

Because it will return as the days passby.

Get up and be inspired.

MOMENTS

Every moment of the day has its own worth.

Morning brings happiness and hope.

The afternoon brings with it feelings of love and devotion.

The night is a time for rest and reflection.

Every day of your life,

I hope you find and enjoy all of these moments.

FOR YOU

Never blame a single day in your life.

Happiness comes from good days and good times with good people.

In addition to bad days, mishaps, and misfortune.

Only disappointments and disapprovals.

Add your experiences together,

Both are extremely important in life.

Ride with God.

He'll keep making things better for you.

AN EVENING REFLECTION FOR YOU

After hearing so much about you,

It only took me a few days to realize what kind of heart you have.

You are a wonderful creature.

The person who not only knows how to care for animals,

But also for humans.

Such a kind-hearted creature is difficult to come by.

That is why everyone should learn to draw closer to others before condemning their personalities and characters.

What a world you and I inhabit;

It all seems like a dream to me.

The role of nature's forces, as well as the magical attractive build-up

GET INSPIRED

Between you and me,

Our stars have acknowledged us,

Gave us a reason to admire one another.

And we were so comfortable in each other's company,

That you didn't hesitate to make your heart my home;

A place I will always crave, day and night.

Even the darkness of the night could not keep me from returning home to you.

Yes, you are distinct, calm, and easygoing.

Concentrated, hardworking, God-fearing,

Above all, you have a good heart.

I can now inform the rest of the world that,

That the grayness of a man is unrelated to his age. his hair, his age, but his heart.

GET INSPIRED

Your heart is as new, honest, loving, and caring.

As a freshly plucked hibiscus flower.

From its stem very early in the morning on a dewy morning,

This was an evening reflection for a kind person in your humility.

YOU

I find myself at a loss for words whenever I think of your worth as a human being.

That day, as I watched you cook with such care and passion for the domestic animals,

I wished such a gesture could be replicated,

Made available to man and humanity.

To tell you the truth,

There is something very special about you in the way you stare at objects,

With such passion, love, and full concentration,

As if you won't let go of the objects of admiration,

It's very sweet of you.

It's the purity of the heart for me,

That makes a good man.

For he is lovely in his own right,

GET INSPIRED

Not because of his physical appearance or material possessions,

Like a full-fledged garden.

May your heart never age.

Though life is like a baby's gable.

It's extremely difficult to comprehend.

Independently perplexing,

Much like an adult's decision.

Similarly, while friendship may be right in front of us,

It cannot flow successfully if the heart is unwilling.

But when we're in the right relationship, things gradually fall into place.

FRIENDSHIP

Meeting you is like discovering a new song,

And floating while listening to the song.

The melody is still hummed non-stop,

Hoping not to be disturbed.

Until one gets into the lyrics,

You're one song that will never go out of tune with me,

With such a lovely tune,

Allow me to be your friend to reckon with

FRIENDSHIP

A gold gift is costly.

A monetary gift is precious.

Roses and lilies make lovely gifts.

However, the gift of you as a friend is priceless.

Thank you for allowing me to live in your heart.

As a friend in need and indeed.

YOU ARE UNIQUE

Take a break, pause for a moment.

Then look at your palms, and tell me what you see.

Certainly you will see lines that can't be erased, right?

You have nothing to be concerned about,

Because the greatest of all is a pure, loving heart,

Which lives within you.

As a result, celebrate your uniqueness,

Because you are magnificently created.

Take pride in your individuality because you were designed for greatness.

Continue to thrive and rule your world.

God's plans for you and your life can never be undone,

So be at rest and assured of a happy life.

MY WORLD, THE WORLD

It's time to face some realities.

That one's world is distinct from the global world,

So one can create his or her own world and fit it into the global world.

My world is how I am able to function,

To mold my attitudes and control my emotions,

Adjust my behavioral patterns, pay attention to my perceptions, and reconsider my worldview.

Disregard what I met in the world which is evil.

Recognizing that my world cannot be your world,

Let my world be mine.

Not the world's world.

DREAMS

While cowards sleep and snore all night,

Great people such as yourself stay awake and dream dreams.

Dreams come to visit us while we sleep.

And prepare our minds for the future.

Martin Luther King, Jr. had a dream that he shared with the world, and it finally came true after 40 years,

After his departure from Earth.

Do you have any dreams?

What is the nature of your dream(s)?

Nonetheless, God is truly gracious because He wakes us up every day,

In addition, provides us with every opportunity to make our dreams come true.

REMAIN BLESSED

May your blessings be as countless Abraham's seeds.

May your dreams come true like Obama's.

Allow your adversaries to lack weapons, as George Bush did.

May your opponents suffer the same fate as McCain.

May all those who speak ill of you perish,

As Paul Biya's government is perplexed,

May your hand always be open.

Like Mother Theresa of blessed memory.

May you be an encourager as well as an aspirant, and light bearer,

Such as Helen Nohgwe Yogo.

May you become as well-known as Pope John Paul II...

Continue to be blessed,

And may God continue to bless you,

Amen.

MY SMILE

I am sending you 1,000 smiles.

Choose one and smile for me today.

Keep the remaining 999 smiles in your pillowcase (s),

Choose one every morning when you get out of bed.

And smile for the day because I want you to smile all the time.

Your smiles could be what a stranger on the street or in the office needs.

On the way to school, farm, car, church, bus, plane, hospital, etc., needs to brighten his/her day.

DID YOU KNOW

How does humor assist us in thinking outside the box?

Is it true that the average child laughs 400 times per day?

Is it true that the average adult only laughs 15 times per day?

What happens to the other 385 laughs?

Laugh as you read this to get to 16 laughs.

And consider what you'll do to cover up the remaining 384 laughs.

DO YOU

Do you know the connection between your two eyes?

Did you know they both blink at the same time?

Do you realize they cry together with one more tear?

Know that they see a lot of things together?

Do you know they sleep deeply together?

Know that even though they never see each other,

They work in tandem at all times T.

Relationships should model these characteristics.

If this were not the case, life would be hell with friends as inconveniences.

CHILDREN

They may appear to be small, tender, and fragile.

Helpless, defenseless, and in need.

Don't dismiss them as shallow.

They contain potentials.

Correctly guide them, tolerate them moderately,

And assist them in discovering who they truly are.

TAKING INITIATIVES WITH NAMES

HELEN

H= Hopeful; showing a desire for something.

E= Eloquent; speaking beautifully and clearly.

L= Lively; exciting and intellectually stimulating.

E= Elegant; stylish, graceful, simple, concise and neat in appearance.

N= Nice; pleasing to look at, showing courtesy.

SIMON

S= Simple; easy to be understood quickly.

I= Iconic; characterized by fame, admiration.

M= Magnificent; impressive, exceptional good of its kind.

O= Objective; free from bias.

N= Noble; having excellent moral character.

ROGER

R= Reactive; tending to react to events or situations rather than initiating them.

O= Officious; eager to give unwanted help or advice

G= Generous; willing to give money or time freely

E= Eristic; fond of argument.

R= Rational; reasonable and sensible.

BENEDICT

B= Bold; fearless, adventurous and daring.

E= Expensive; costing a lot.

N= Narrative; able to give a clear account of something.

E= Excellent; extremely good.

D= Decisive; able to make definite decisions.

I= Inventive; good at creating new things.

C= Charming; having the power to attract people.

T=Tactical; showing skillful planning to accomplish something.

YARI

Y= Yare; quick and lively.

A= Able; capable and talented.

R= Respectful; showing respect for all.

I= Idealistic; somebody who abides by high standards and principles.

CHRISTOPHER

C= Calm; not anxious, not violent.

H= Hard working; tending to work industriously.

R=Responsible; reliable base on trustworthiness and conscientiousness.

I=Impressive; causing admiration and respect.

S=Systematic; well organized.

T=Tough; possessing great endurance.

O=Observant; paying sure and careful attention that little or nothing is unnoticed.

P=Peaceful; quiet and calm.

H=Honest; expressing or embodying the truth.

E=Equable; calm and not easily disturbed.

R=Reliable; able to be trusted to do what is accurate and expected.

LAWRENCE

L=Liable; likely to do something.

A=Accommodative; easily adjust to provide sufficient space to somebody.

W=Wondrous; so good and admirable.

R =Realistic

E=Emotional; easily expressing emotions

N=Neat; orderly in appearance.

C=Courageous; having the ability to face difficulty, uncertainty or pain without being overcome by fear

E=Encouraging; ability to give somebody courage or hope.

DOULAS

D=Devoted; feeling or showing great love/loyalty to somebody.

O=Optimistic; somebody with positive attitude

U=Upgradable; somebody thatimproves.

L=Lighter; a person that lights or illuminates.

A=Ardent; feeling great passion, showing enthusiasm.

S=Sagacious; wise or shrewd; having a profound knowledge and understanding about the world.

JUSTINA

J=Justifiable; capable of being shown as reasonable.

U=Understanding; ability to express sympathy and empathy to someone.

S=Smart; well-groomed and clever.

T=Talented; having natural ability to do things.

I=Introspective; ability to examine your feelings.

N=Negotiable; open to discussion

A=Attractive; good looking.

NDRENAH (My Mama's unique name)

N=Noiseless; doesn't talk unnecessarily, makes no unpleasant sound.

D=Decent; kindly, tolerant and likeable.

R=Respectable; having a good reputation and character

N=Natural; normal as a mother, wife, friend as one would expect

A=Appreciative; gives due thanks or praise always.

H=Holy; good, pure, follows rules always.

JULIE

J=Jovial; full of good humor…

U=Unanimous; having or showing complete agreement…

L=Liberal; generous, tolerant…

I=Imaginative; ability to create or having mental pictures of positive outcomes…

E=Eloquent; ability to speak clearly…

PETER

P=Powerful; having great strength and influence…

E=Exceptional; unusual, remarkable…

T=Temporal; ability to keep things lasting…

E=Equalitarian; a person who wants things to either be the same or equal…

R=Regardful; thinking and caring about cost…

HAPPINESS

H=Harmless; not dangerous and can not cause any harm…

A=Apparent; easy to see, evident …

P=Promising; likely to be good…

P=Prominent; easily seen, famous, standing out…

I=Irascible; easily made angry.

N=Noticeable; easily noticed.

E=Expectant; full of hopes and expectations.

S=Succulent; juicy, attractive.

S=Sufficient; just enough, satisfied…

HOLINESS

H=Hopeful; likely to be successful, pleasant.

O=Organized; having ability to plan well, efficient and well-arranged.

L=Lifelike; full of life.

I=Iridescent; always shinning or glittering…

N=Nourishing; ability to give the body what is necessary for health and growth.

E=Expedient; convenient or advisable.

S=Suggestible; ability to tell one's mind.

S=Suitable; right or appropriate.

YOGO

Y=Yuppie; young, ambitious and a professional…

O=Open; allowing his inside to be seen

G=Godly; religious man and father.

WE ALL NEED HELP

Every day as I walk down the streets,

I see thousands of people looking for some sort of assistance.

Some people need financial assistance,

While others need employment,

Women need good husbands.

Men look for faithful wives.

Parents should pray for godly children.

Politicians strive for more nominations.

Business magnates compete for new contracts.

Teachers are looking forward to higher pay.

The elderly pray for strength and assistance.

Babies cry out to be fed, suckled, and pampered.

Blind men search for their sticks.

GET INSPIRED

Physically challenged people sought assistance.

Pastors are on the lookout for new members.

The masses yearn for a change in power.

Scholars are looking forward to the approaching holidays.

Professors opt for time off.

Agriculturalists strive for favorable weather.

Farmers strike for recognition and appreciation of their products

I pray for good leadership.

Communism, Unionism, Solidarity, Love, Peace, and Acceptance

While God patiently awaits the transformation of man's wicked heart,

We all need help.

LOVE

I am the one you are looking for.

When you share me, you'll have me.

Accept me and allow me to manifest my worth in you.

Look for me nowhere else.

For you will not find me in another place;

I was placed in you for your benefit.

You'll have me if you find me.

Why have you decided to bury me within you and expect to see me in others when I was meant to be shared and experienced by all?

That is not how I operate.

When will you begin to share me?

You will start to like me.

Begin today and stop crying.

GET INSPIRED

You'll be completed once you have me.

I am the pinnacle of all virtues.

My name is LOVE, and some people call me CHARITY.

And as you are probably aware, charity begins at home,

So I am love, and I live in you.

HAPPINESS

My surroundings are pleasant when I am present.

Oh! It becomes sad and sour when I am absent.

Smiles, joyous shouts, and rejoicing fill the air in my presence.

Hmmm! Things fall apart when I take a French leave.

My French leave in an English style is just a test to see if you can withstand Osama Bin Laden.

Because you didn't have to look at the German soldiers or fear the battalions as they marched by,

Because the Russians will never leave, no matter what.

The Gentiles may exist solely to strengthen the Israelites.

Assuring that the Egyptians we see today will no longer be seen tomorrow...

Then I, Happiness, will reappear,

To reclaim my proper place in your lives.

BLACKLEADERS

Oh! What kind of nations are you constructing for us, our leaders?

Is it a nation?

Where will we learn about our lefts and rights?

Is it a country where there would be democracy, love, and peace?

Or a nation where we will carry our knives, spoons, forks, nails, pens, and fight for survival of the fittest?

Why, black leaders, have you decided to be dark and black in your hearts?

When you travel by air to other continents,

How do you feel around the world?

When you walk on paved roads?

And how do you feel about graded ground?

Why don't you emulate all of these and give those who voted

you into power a taste of their choice?

How long will you tolerate being referred to as "black monkeys", black leaders?

Is it the color that makes a difference?

Or the initiative and willingness to do what you should do?

This is a fact that needs to be addressed again.

Our black leaders' stomachs continue to expand,

As their followers trek for days to their respective villages.

Oh no, what a government!

Our black leaders have devised flamboyant ten-points agendas;

"Grand ambitions"

Operation Health for All in 2015;

Nonetheless, mothers and children perish on our planets.

Because of a scarcity of basic primary health care services.

GET INSPIRED

This is unfathomable, black leaders!

I pray you have conscience.

Our black leaders want to stay in power until thy kingdom come,

Because they can't care for only children and rural people,

And if they could, life would be more meaningful and promising for the society.

Our black leaders sponsor their children abroad.

And encourage the common man's children to steal, violate,

And have sexual affairs with them in order to benefit from the National cakes,

Jesus, what a pity!

I pray for our black leaders to not be defined by the color of their skin.

You can make a difference if your heart and leadership style reflect that.

GET INSPIRED

I have the ability to effect change.

We can all help to make a difference.

It must start now, with me, with you, with us.

Our black leaders,

We'd be delighted to call you.

Leaders, not black leaders

Remove the adjective "black" if you prefer.

Borrow no color at all,

Simply be our leaders, not rulers, but people's leaders.

For the people, by the people.

As fathers/mothers to their children,

May God bless our leaders.

Amen.

WHEN THE TIME COMES

Everything has its own time.
The time has come for me to make a change.

I will undoubtedly attend.
It is a time ordained by God,
It appears far away, but it is not,
And it will happen in God's time.

I am preparing morally, physically, spiritually,
Academically, socially, economically, psychologically,
Culturally, and intellectually.
These and other tools will I use God's willing,
To create a community of communism, love, and peace.

Oneness, Equity, and Empowerment,
Freedom of expression, press, and talent.

GET INSPIRED

When the time comes,

It will be a no man's land.

Where kind people will be,

Prepared to chase away evildoers,

Where children will be reminded of their rich cultural heritage.

And how to put their socio-cognitive skills to use,

And learn how to get rid of their facades and negative ideographs.

When the time comes,

It will not be all about money or enriching family members,

From the national coffers.

But it will be all about Common Objectives, Common Interests, and Common Perspectives,

Implementing, Evaluating, and Completing Sustainable Community Projects.

For the benefit of all.

BEAUTY

Beauty is relative.

It's appealing, sharp, and flashy.

True men seek inner beauty rather than outer beauty.

Most beautiful women exhibit and express some degree of shyness,

When given the opportunity to show off what they have.

It's amazing just like their worth.

To discover their true beauty

Beauty brings peace, respect, and fulfillment.

No woman is not beautiful;

They are all unique.

In their natural appearance, as created by God.

GET INSPIRED

I pity men who compare women.

Because they are specifically and wonderfully designed for appreciation,

Rather than comparison with others.

Every woman has a unique shape, style, color, size, and taste.

You are free to have whatever you want.

Only when you invest your time, affection, patience, love, respect, and loyalty do you gain a woman.

A lovely lady is calm, humble, gentle, faithful, understanding, and

Above all, she is virtuous,

Making her husband proud.

She makes her husband smile when he wants to cry.

She adores her home and raises her children to be responsible.

WOMAN

She has been referred to as a bouncing baby girl since birth.

She is treated as a piece of joy as a toddler.

She was considered attractive as a child.

She has an iota of admiration as a teen.

She is adored as a flower as an adult.

She becomes a mother as a woman.

What a Creature-Woman!

The universe, a caregiver!

A woman was made from a man.

Nonetheless, she is more modified than a man.

God gave her twice as much as He gave to the man.

She has longer hair, larger breasts, better shape,

A longer life span, nicer nails, and so on.

In everything God gave man, He doubled it for the woman.

A lady is a lady.

Whatever the choice,

Whatever the color, whatever the smile,

Whatever the style, whatever the waist.

She was designed to be productive,

To do great things and to do good things in the garden of life.

You have a daughter in every baby girl.

Every daughter has a sister.

There is an aunty for every sister.

There is a friend in every aunty.

There is a wife in every friend.

GET INSPIRED

There is a mother in that wife.

And there is a woman in every mother.

As a result, a woman is a woman.

I AM PROUD TO BE A WOMAN.

I am a person.

I am a lady.

I don't have any regrets.

I was created and was born as a woman.

If I weren't a woman, I'd be a man.

I'm curious about who I would have been,

Even though women differ,

In some way or another,

Changing from one form to another.

I am proud to be a woman in any shape or form.

Aside from every successful man,

There is a possible lady.

Men cannot exist without women.

GET INSPIRED

Appropriately satisfy their desire,

Better choices are made,

When women are consulted.

Without women, there won't be care and procreation.

In the absence of female breasts,

Babies will be properly fed from artificial sources.

Without a woman on the planet,

There is no true companion for a man.

A woman is an essential member and component of life.

Forget about the so-called bad or wicked women;

It's because they don't know what they're doing.

Their worth and who they were created to be,

I am only pleased I was born a woman.

MY MOTHER

Muertoh (Princess) Ndrenah is her unique name.
I've never seen her twin before.

She gave me life and then let me be part of this world.
She cared for me like an egg without a hen.
She fed me for as long as I wanted with her breasts,
Despite thick and thin

She gave me a hopeful smile.
She never stopped believing in me,
To be a good child and a good woman,
And saying that God is watching me.

Keep up your good work,
And everything will be fine.

GET INSPIRED

My mother is God's best gift to me;

She is a virtuous woman in her character, behavior,

Words, and actions.

She is much more than a mother to everyone.

When I need money and she is unable to provide it,

She would sell items.

She gives enough food when I cry for it.

When I need a friend, she lends me her ears.

Open her arms and protect me from the cold.

To shield me from the torrential rain and wind,

She beats me up when I'm wrong and praises me when I'm good.

As a child, she held my hand and taught me to look up to God.

She taught me how to pray,

Shared her love with me,

And encouraged me to be a better person.

I strive to be a beacon of light in everything I do and preach.

The candle she lit for me on my baptism day is still burning today.

My heart is leading the way for others.

She asked me to let my light shine until she placed the candle in my hands.

Meet my Creator, who will bless me.

Muertoh (Princess) Ndrenah Suefue is my mother's name.

ME

I am who I am because He created me.

When I realized I was myself Because I was created

I grinned and thanked God.

I am not you.

I must always be myself.

He created you and me.

As a result of which both of us,

Will shape the universe.

You play your part, and I play mine.

I use my voice as myself.

To make music for broken heart,

Troubled souls and thanks to God.

Grow children and speak positively about the future.

As for me, I write to inspire others.

GET INSPIRED

And speak for those who cannot.

I fill in the gaps for others.

In the event of a positive outcome,

I beg you to be you,

And I will be me,

So that, together, we can build a world,

Where everyone feels a sense of belonging.

You can achieve whatever you set your mind to.

When it comes to the willingness to do something,

Yes, you can, and you should keep trying.

Consider those who invented and made discoveries.

They all began like you and me.

If only we could take a step forward without looking back.

Then, and yes, you can...

BE HAPPY

Don't be discouraged if you don't understand the situations you find yourself in;

Instead, keep your head up and go ahead;

Be happy.

Trouble days do not last long;

They only appear at night,

And by morning, joy comes to cheer.

You're up, good success is real, and you should be happy.

I WAS ONCE LIKE YOU

I used to feel terrible,

When my world appeared to be crumbling at that point.

When all hope appeared to be lost and endless,

Until I had to confront the reality that,

There are ups and downs in life.

Today's sweetness, tomorrow's bitterness ,

Today's friends are tomorrow's enemies,

Today's helpers are evolving into opportunists - manipulators.

That life has a sweet, sour, and flavorless side.

I used to be like you...

I questioned whether I would ever make it in this life.

I looked for my abilities, talents, and skills.

I did a lot of good odd jobs and rendered services.

However, I found no pleasure in them because I had no passion for them.

The many people I served never appreciated me.

I failed and was unhappy despite my best efforts to make it on my own.

I then conducted an inner search and thought within myself.

Where did I come from, who created me, and why?

I saw my Creator, my Source, smiling at me there.

So, without hesitation, I ran to Him in prayer and praise,

Surrendering everything to Him and asking for forgiveness.

Not too long after, I discovered my hidden talents that had been buried, hidden, and suppressed within me for years.

All due to self-ignorance and negligence.

GET INSPIRED

Don't worry; I was once like you...

If and only if you could take a break from your extremely busy,

And demanding schedule to think like I did,

Then you will discover the solutions to your wealth and health problems.

A kind of wealth reserved solely for you...

I used to be like you...

You are sitting on your potentials, possessions, and opportunities.

God's gifts are like a rare breed to behold.

Look deeper; it's all deposited deep within you.

That money you require.

Those resources you fantasize about.

That vision you had.

GET INSPIRED

You're looking for a husband/wife.
That enterprise you must establish.
That leader you aspire to be.
Hey! They are all within you.

Sleeper, wake up!
Get up, dreamer!
Be cheerful, beggar!
A community needs you;
I used to be like you...

YOU NEED IT

Knowledge illuminates the path and lightens your burdens.

It could be how to proceed,

Or how to deal with an issue you don't want to share with anyone.

Whatever the case may be,

Knowledge is needed.

Yes, you need it.

Knowledge, according to some, is power.

It is wealth to others.

It represents strength to them.

It is energy to us.

It enlightens mothers.

It gives elders power.

It encourages fathers.

It inspires and gives hope to children.

It provides guidance to a blind man.

It is seen by an orphan as a succor. It indicates to me

Though different people may have different perspectives,

On what knowledge means to them.

You need it...

HARDTIMES

When adversity comes your way,

It implies that good times are on their way.

It is very close to your location.

Maintain your focus, stand firm, and grab your package.

Do not be put off by hard times.

When you're having a good time,

Rather than when you're having a bad time.

When your package of good times arrives at your door,

Smile and let it in.

Allow your faith to go open the door,

Answer, saying "You're welcome good times, I've been expecting you,

What's kept you from coming all these years?"

Then say, "never mind, I'm glad you're here now, though I'm

Overjoyed to see you,

Because I knew you are definitely going to knock on my door."

HOW ABOUT YOU?

I was once in the dark,

In a tunnel with no light,

Trying to live my life as I had desired.

I suddenly realized that it wasn't all about me,

But what I can offer to the community,

That had received me as a child,

To raise me into an adult intellectual woman.

So I decided to pay them a price.

And to others, please allow my generation,

I know there was a time when I was like that.

I began teaching, singing, and designing,

Participating in community service,

Sharing love and showing appreciation to others

While doing these,

I discovered my talent in Creative Writing

I began investing my time and energy as God directed.

Strength, resources, and power

I even forego spending time with some friends,

And cancel all unnecessary outings and shows.

To ensure that God's plan for me is carried out.

As a result, the articles you're reading,

The books you've probably read or heard of,

Songs you've probably heard,

And stories you've probably heard or watched as drama in videos,

Were created, written, and produced by me as God directed.

How about you?

I'd like to ask.

HE LIVES IN ME

I arrived from somewhere.

I was sent for a reason.

I was created for a specific purpose.

My current life is not mine.

I can't add or subtract anything,

From that which I am and was destined to be.

There is a power within me that can be harnessed.

If you want, it can work for you as well.

It is a Spirit who does it,

And He lives within me.

It brings me joy and happiness,

And guides every decision I make on a daily basis.

It neither sleeps nor slumbers.

It speaks to me and guides my steps.

He is capable of doing the same for you (Psalm 121)

I get up every day because it says so,

And I go to sleep at night because He leads.

It is a Good Spirit;

It has emotion, will, and focus,

And all of these occur,

Because I am connected to my Source,

The Creator.

As a result,

He lives in me,

That which is greater.

Than that which is Greatest than that which is in the world?

The Holy Spirit.

LIFE- YOUR LIFE

Your greatest adversary is yourself.

It stands out as either discouraging or encouraging.

Make your life out of your life,

Not from the food you have, the good fortune to eat on a daily basis,

Nor from the clothes you've been blessed with,

Nor the insults you receive from others,

Nor the way you appear.

Let no one blame you for your life,

Now, you must understand who you truly are.

Thus, life is all about you and how you decide to live your life.

NOT BY MY STATURE

My age is not proportional to my physical make-up,

And I thank God for molding me in this manner for His perfect will.

My life does not depend or lie on my status.

Rather, it operates from the openness, readiness, and purity of my heart.

I am the person God created me to be.

Not because of my current situation.

Look not at my stature,

But at what He has done through me,

Because His words must be fulfilled accordingly.

For if you look at my stature,

You run the risk of not finding anything.

Why not jump right into my challenges?

GET INSPIRED

To see how long I've been wandering in the wilderness of life ,

For adequate preparations and sanctification,

You'll believe that a woman's greatness does not lie in her status-quo,

But in God's plan for that soul.

It was a lot of fun going through life's wilderness and traffic jams,

In the Light of God,

Just to be well prepared to emerge a winner,

A superstar for a brighter future.

COMMUNICATION

Communication can be either positive or negative.

When it's negative, it becomes deceptive,

And listeners only enjoy it for a short time.

Positive communication produces smiles and joys,

That last as long as the communicators want,

Because it becomes a part of the speakers.

Do you realize that one of your weaknesses could be a lack of communication?

Every time we speak,

We reveal who we are,

What we intend to do unconsciously,

And sometimes to people we don't want to know our plans,

Opinions, and innermost thoughts.

GET INSPIRED

Communication is a very powerful and sacred tool,

That can be used against oneself,

Based on the facts that one has uttered about oneself,

Personality, friends and relatives.

However, in our daily lives,

We must communicate,

So we can't avoid communication entirely.

In fact, we must be extremely selective and wise,

In our word usage and what people say to us.

Communication is good,

But don't be a victim of poor communication;

Don't say anything until it's absolutely necessary,

Expected, and required of you.

GET INSPIRED

Wise people speak less but listen more intently.

If one keeps a daily record of all one's communication,

One will be astounded to discover that,

Everything the world needs to know and does not need to know about one,

Has already been said,

knowingly or unknowingly.

These may be relevant in communication:

Smiles, gesticulations, signs, symbols, fingers, and eyes.

And the hands, body hair, and legs

Communication does, in fact, come from the heart.

From the mouth to the face and the actions.

Keep an eye on what you say while communicating.

TEARS

These are liquid particles that occasionally fall,

From one's eyes in the shape of a pot.

There are varieties of reasons,

Why humans and animals alike,

Allow these pot-shaped water particles to run down their chicks.

There are love tears.

Happy and tears of happiness.

Sweet melodies' tears.

Tears of joy.

Tears of satisfaction.

Good-surprise tears.

Success tears.

Congratulation tears.

GET INSPIRED

Reconciliation tears.

People shed tears of sorrow,

Sadness, loneliness, and emptiness in the same light.

Frustration, poverty, and an abrupt departure.

Whatever the case may be,

Tears are genuine.

Tears, however, are considered impure by some.

If it is not shared for a good cause,

You don't have to cry when it's not necessary;

Rather, learn through your tears.

It is the best medicine to smile.

Wear a smile to hide your tears.

Our God is not pleased when we cry unnecessarily,

And shed our tears about our situations like those who do not know their God;

He expects us to smile, be bold, and have faith even with teary eyes,

Entrusting everything to Him. For He made tears so we could share them to express our emotions.

MY ONLY FRIEND

I only have one trustworthy friend.

He is the best friend I've ever had.

He is my only friend.

He sees my heart and is aware of my actions.

He tells me what to do,

And what not to do for my own good,

Because He helps me prepare for today,

And plans for tomorrow.

He is the only one who protects me from so-called enemies ,

And wrong paths in life.

He's my most trusted and best friend,

And the most lovely of all my friends.

He covers for my flaws,

And maximizes my key to propel me to the top.

He directs my steps and orders my movements on a daily basis.

I first heard about Him,

Through an assembly of believers on Mount Calvary.

The day I confessed all of my sins and unfaithfulness.

He is the only friend I have inside of me.

We laugh, talk, play, and sleep together,

But no one can see Him except in spirit,

Where He is present and sovereign.

I've never traveled without Him or without His approval,

Because He follows me everywhere I go,

Making sure I'm okay.

GET INSPIRED

I won't go anywhere without Him by my side,

Because he is my most senior companion,

He is the most compassionate, faithfully faithful,

And trustworthy friend I've ever had and have free access to.

His thoughts for me are always of joy, love, prosperity.

His preservation is over me.

He has never gossiped about me or laughed at me.

He shields me and encourages me.

He helps me with everything I need.

I've shared Him with many people,

But His love for us all has never wavered.

They're always and have remained constant throughout the years.

His name is Lord Jesus Christ.

A BIRTHDAY GIFT FOR YOU

I'd like to offer you a happy birthday gift,
But I'm not sure what you'll value the most on this special day,
In your life.

I have a lovely photo of myself,
Some lovely roses and lilies,
And an amazing designer's basket filled with my undying love

I intend to send this lovely photograph,
But, on second thought,
I realized that if I send this photo,
You will only be able to see me.
As I turned my attention,
To the lovely Roses and Lilies I carefully plucked,
It got done on me that these precious flowers may wither,
And die before reaching you at your birthday party.

And you won't be able to admire and enjoy the flavor,

And such natural beauty of the flowers I personally gathered for you on such a special occasion,

Since I will not be present,

This is a very special day.

Turning around, I noticed the designer's basket labeled,

"Yogo's Fashion,"

And I immediately thought of sending it to you.

Oh no!

There was a small opening at basket,

Hmmm.

I'm almost gave up on sending you any birthday gifts,

And just relax my nerves,

It occurred to me that you would need more than the three gifts

GET INSPIRED

Yes, I smiled to myself,

As I've been thinking all along,

Of what you've loved; These thoughts rolled down my head;

Why not share it with your friend?

On such a one-year celebration and always.

Nobody else will think of such priceless gifts.

Make a difference among all the gift givers.

Your gift should be the gift of pure love,

I jumped up, excitedly grabbing the Designer's basket,

Labeled "Yogo's Fashion."

I repaired the tiny hold in the middle.

Fitted the lovely roses and lilies,

I attached a lovely photo and wrote a brief note of encouragement.

I kissed it with my love and finally delivered the gifts to you.

GET INSPIRED

After the exercise,

I felt as if I had given out a special and one-of-a-kind gift,

On a friend's birthday and always.

I wrote in my brief note,

“Here's a photo,"

Have it, keep it, and feel her presence on your birthday,

And always collect these roses and lilies,

Water them every morning and evening,

And as for the Basket,

Do as you please,

But guard it jealously and share it with my Love.

As I wish you a Merry and a Happy Birthday for many more years,

God bless you.

CATCH UP

So, what are you waiting for?

So, who are you waiting for?

Don't you realize that time waits for no one?

Catch up with time!

You may believe that everything is lost.

Because of your poor academic background,

Because of your poor family background,

Because of your poor health,

Don't you realize there is a God?

Who has instilled so much in you?

Why do you cry yourself to sleep with a heavy heart?

When beggars became presidents

GET INSPIRED

Paupers have become ministers.

Prostitutes have risen to the position of First Ladies.

Hey! It is not for you to judge yourself,

Nor should you be depressed,

Or have low self-esteem.

There is certainly hope for your case.

Please hear me now,

Wherever you are,

Whatever you're doing right now.

Whatever you do,

Do it well,

With devotion and love.

Spread your seeds everywhere.

GET INSPIRED

Determine what you can do best with your certificates,

Diplomas, and degrees.

You will always go to school in order to advance and improve yourself.

Your current state is irrelevant.

What you can do today is what matters.

I see you reading this book becoming the eye-opener for a needy family,

The light that some people will need to shine.

Do not kill it.

Catch up with time.

FACTS TO REMEMBER AS WE GO THROUGH LIFE'S TRAFFIC JAMS

1) God changes time and season if you choose to work according to His calendar for your life, which I believe is the best option to rely on throughout one's life on Earth.

2) Time and chance are the facts about development and attainment of one's destiny.

3) Life is like a game; depending on how you want to end it, you can play it safe, rough, or go risky.

4) You cannot tell your life stories better if you lack experiences.

5) When you are lonely, it is the perfect time to ask God who you are and who He created you to be.

6) Life is not constant. As a result, a successful life should be guided by absolute principles, phases, determinations, and accomplishments.

7) If you must cry in life, cry in such a unique way that anyone who hears your cry will be able to recognize you from your cry.

8) Cook deliciously for your husband, keep his clothes and the house clean, neat, and appealing at all times, provide the best sexual satisfaction for him, and always pray for him. Everything else will fall into place.

9) All women seek security, material possessions, and respect.

10) Never underestimate a child, regardless of age or gender. Give them the chance, and you'll be amazed at their abilities, skills, and capabilities.

11) Childhood is the most mysterious stage in a person's life. At this point, a lot is being done both consciously and

unconsciously, and very few adult humans remember what it was like to be a child.

12) My mother taught me honesty, honor, purity, fidelity, humility, generosity, charity, meekness, open-mindedness, and love.

13) A life must always have plans A, B, C, and D. When plan A is known, don't be afraid to switch to plan B and then plan C if plan A fails, but don't reveal plan D to someone Unless otherwise, so that you do not lose everything.

14) Depending on your beliefs, God is the Master Planner and you are the servant planner.

15) Most men lie about their salaries, while most women lie about their ages.

16) Younger men preach and talk about love to the women they date, whereas older men show, express, and care for the women they date and do less talking.

17) For most teenagers and adolescents, the game is love, the deal is sexual intercourse, and the result is sudden separation, destruction of divine purpose, unwanted pregnancy and passing on to the next vulnerable teen.

18) True intimacy begins with attraction, followed by the individual's personality as others fall into place.

19) A cheap woman is one who does not respond with a NO, whereas an expensive and quality woman is one who knows when to say NO and when to say YES, or HELLO, EXCUSE ME! DO YOU THINK IT COULD HAVE BEEN THIS WAY? OR WHAT DO YOU THINK?

20) If you're not sure what to say in public, don't say anything; and if you must, just smile.

21) If you want to protect your marriage, avoid criticizing your partner at all costs. Instead, make quality time and space for mutual dialogue and teachings as needed.

22) Allow for feedback when appreciating your acts and actions, but don't expect positive feedback all the time.

23) Marriage is first and foremost a Holy contract, then a Sacred contract, and finally a Social contract between two physically, psychologically, and emotionally fit, sound man and woman in the university of eternity, faculty of mutual benefits, department of love and agreement, no supervisors as malice and beatings, in fulfillment for a certificate of no graduation with a carrying over of sometimes children.

24) No insane person is a waste to society.

25) One truth about life is that you cannot deceive anyone forever, except yourself.

26) The one person you should try to know the best is yourself, because if you want to make a difference in the world, you should start with the person you know best, who is supposed to be no one else but yourself.

27) Because human hearts are very wicked and unpredictable, never expect good judgments or rewards from anyone; instead, look up to God, the only true and Good and Perfect Judge.

28) Do what you ought to do, which must be right, and avoid everything that ought not to be done, which is evil.

29) Make life easy and gradual, because there is no shortcut to life.

30) Every human's destiny is unique and peculiar, regardless of social stratification.

31) Education is a long-term investment in an unpredicted bank account with guaranteed returns in any currency chosen by the investor. All you have to do as an investor is take the risk and keep saving so that when you are gone, it will speak for you if you saved in the right bank.

32) Nature's work is breathtaking. Life is like a tree; when the old shoots die, the new ones sprout. So, as you walk around the graveyards, pay attention to what the people there are saying: "As you are, so I was, as I am, so you shall be."

Such is life.

33) It is in the nature of women to cry out their hurts, and it is in the nature of men to make sound decisions when situations are beyond their control.

34) A woman was born to be happy; to be productive in life's valley, to do good and to be useful to humanity.

35) When one marries and becomes attached to the ordained rightful partner of his/her choice, marriage becomes the sweetest vacation in life.

36) It's a good thing that ends well.

37) Violence is the most ineffective weapon in any battle.

38) Violence breeds conflict and crisis, which in turn breed massive hatred and destruction.

39) The most difficult expression in any language is "I'm sorry".

40) Out of the millions of people we interact with on a daily basis, we have complete control over who we allow into our lives and who we do not.

41) When things get tough, remember that good fortune is just around the corner.

42) Misfortunes frequently come our way, but let us consider the great future that comes our way in life after each misfortune.

43) A wicked woman is as dangerous as the most dangerous viper, whereas a good woman is as soft and harmless as a dove.

44) Beauty is flashy, but attitude is authentic.

45) If you want to know how or what your wife will look like when she is forty or older, ask for a picture of your mother-in-law at that age or imagine your mother-in-law at forty if you haven't met her yet.

46) If you truly want to admire your woman's nature, do so very early in the morning before she puts on her mask.

47) A man's attractiveness is determined by his heart, not his pocket, and how much he can make you scream his name all night.

48) Dreaming is free, but making your dreams a reality requires tact.

49) Despite the fact that there is a clear distinction between sight and vision, they are brother and sister.

50) As far back as I can remember in world history, each generation had a specific goal in mind. For example, from 1920 to 1940, our fore-fathers worked for Civilization and a better life; from 1940 to 1960, they fought in World War II. They fought for Freedom and Liberation, they invested in Education and Technology from 1960 to 1980, but parents from 1980 to the present do not know what they are aiming for. However, one could argue that they have created Corruption, Bribery, Violence, and Bad Governance on a scale that the world has never seen before.

BONUSES

True love can be experienced when two souls are inexplicably connected. But lust is when he/she loves your body for the time being. Though, this doesn´t rule out the power of physical chemistry. Remember love is a beautiful thing, don´t get it twisted.

And don´t get it twisted between love, lust and a fling. It requires an experience with Divine love (God´s Love) first before discerning whether another mortal truly loves you, is lusting after you or just wants a fling with you.

A woman´s treasures doesn´t lies in a man´s pocket, likewise, a man´s destiny doesn´t lies in-between the legs of a woman.

It takes a foolish man to be dragged by a woman because of intimacy, same way it takes a foolish woman to think that, if she doesn´t do the odds to bewitch a man, she cannot live a profitable life.

When interest is the rationale behind support, ignorance and blindness to failed and malfunctioning systems are inevitable.

In the mystery of life, you must not push away someone from the queue in order to step in.

In the exercise of solidarity, personal expected gains are signals that, your solidarity gestures were masked.

There will always be the ´road not travelled by some´ or missed opportunities, however we can always find help along the way as we make decisions.

Love is the only undisputable healing factor when it comes to the relationship between the created universe and the established human system.

Getting into trouble doesn´t really make you troublesome. Unless you are intentional in doing so. Hence once you get into trouble, carry out a vivid assessment to ascertain what happened and address it. Accept the situation, assume responsibility and think!

www.ingramcontent.com/pod-product-compliance
Lightning Source LLC
LaVergne TN
LVHW050319160826
845677LV00014B/3478